I0799590

WonderWorks

Decodable Reader

Unit 6

McGraw Hill

Contents

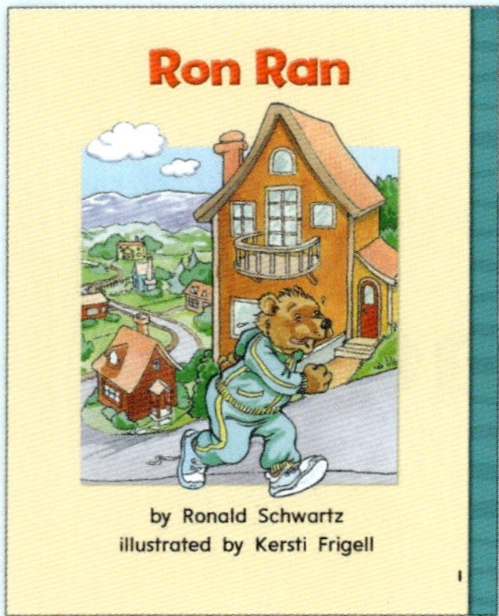
Ron Ran
by Ronald Schwartz
illustrated by Kersti Frigell
1

Little Tab Can Sit
by Nina Adams
illustrated by Deborah Colvin Borgo
9

Can We Pack It?
by Nate Clayton
17

Ron Ran

by Ronald Schwartz
illustrated by Kersti Frigell

Ron ran and ran.
Ron did not sit.

Ron ran and ran.
Ron did not like it.

Ron ran and ran.
Ron ran to the top.

Ron can not go on.
He can sit and sit.

Can Ron fit in it?
Ron can fit in it!

Ron sat **with** Rat.
Ron, you can fit!

Little Tab Can Sit

by Nina Adams

illustrated by Deborah Colvin Borgo

Tan Tab **is** a **little** pet.
Tan Tab **is** not bad.

Bob had Tan Tab sit.
Tan Tab sat and sat.

Bob can pet Tan Tab.
See Bob pet Tan Tab.

Bob had Tan Tab sit.

Little Tab sat and sat.

Bob sat a lot.
Tan Tab sat a lot.

Bob let Tab hop on his lap.
Little Tab sat on Bob.

Can We Pack It?

by Nate Clayton

PR Image Factory/Shutterstock

Tom Grill/Photographer's Choice RF/Getty Images

Kim can pack a can.

She can pack it in a sack.

Lane Oatey/Blue Jean Images/Getty Images

Nick can pack a rock.
He can set it in the sack.

PR Image Factory/Shutterstock

Deb can go see Pop.
Deb can pack Jack.

Marta Nardini/Flickr/Getty Images

Mack can kick, kick, kick.
Mack can pack it in a sack.

Big Cheese Photo/SuperStock

Can Dad pack it up?
Dad can pack, pack, pack it.

Ronnie Kaufman/Corbis/Getty Images

It **was** a lot to pack!

Unit 6

Word Count: 57

Decodable Words

Target Phonics Elements: Consonants /f/*f*, /r/*r*
fit, ran, Rat, Ron
Review: *can, did, in, it, not, on, sat, sit, top*

High-Frequency Words

he, with
Review: *and, go, like, the, to, you*

Word Count: 65

Decodable Words

Target Phonics Elements: Initial and Final /b/*b*, Consonant /l/*l*
bad, Bob, lap, let, lot, Tab
Review: *can, had, hop, not, on, pet, sat, sit, tan*

High-Frequency Words

is, little
Review: *a, and, see*

Week 3 • *Can We Pack It?* .... page 17

Word Count: 66

Decodable Words

Target Phonics Elements: Initial /k/*k*, Digraph *ck*
Jack, kick, Kim, Mack, Nick, pack, rock, sack
Review: *can, Dad, Deb, did, in, it, lot, Pop, set*

High-Frequency Words

she, was
Review: *a, go, he, the, to, see, we*

Decoding skills taught to date:

Consonants /m/*m*, /s/*s*, /p/*p*, /t/*t*; Short *a*; Short *i*; Initial and Final /n/*n*; Initial /k/*c*; Short *o*; Initial and Final /d/*d*; Consonant /h/*h*; Short *e*; Blends *sn, sp, st*; Consonants /f/*f*, /r/*r*; Initial and Final /b/*b*; Consonant /l/*l*; Initial /k/*k*; Digraph *ck*